W9-BKN-310

LES CHATS
de Paris

{ Cats in Paris }

BARNABY CONRAD III

CHRONICLE BOOKS
SAN FRANCISCO

FOR PERRINE, GEORGIE, JEAN-CLAUDE,
WALTER, MANUEL, AND MADELEINE, WITH
LOVE AND GRATITUDE

Copyright ©1996 by Barnaby Conrad III.
See credits p.69 for individual copyrights
of the photographs.

All rights reserved. No part of this book may
be reproduced without written permission
from the Publisher.

Printed in Singapore.

Book and cover design:
Jilly Simons, Concrete, Chicago

Library of Congress Cataloging-in-Publication Data:
Conrad, Barnaby, 1952–
Les Chats de Paris / [photographs compiled]
by Barnaby Conrad III.
p. cm.
ISBN 0-8118-1186-7
1. Photography of cats. 2. Photography, Artistic.
3. Cats—Pictorial works.
4. Paris (France)—Pictorial works.   I. Title.
TR729.C3C66 1996
779'.32—dc20   95-23318
                                CIP

Distributed in Canada by Raincoast Books
8680 Cambie Street
Vancouver, B.C. V6P 6M9

10 9 8 7 6 5 4 3 2

Chronicle Books
85 Second Street
San Francisco, CA 94105

Web Site: www.chronbooks.com

INTRODUCTION

CATS PURSUE SECRETIVE AND ECCENTRIC LIVES IN PARIS. Rarely seen in the streets by day, they slumber in boudoirs or peer quizzically from the windows of flower and antique shops. At night they catch mice in bakeries, slip silently down cobblestone alleys, and prowl the rooftops, yowling for assignations. Or they stay home and pay attention to a lucky human: *Caress me, then feed me, and I'll purr.* If dogs represent the solid bourgeois aspects of Paris, cats might be seen as alluring emissaries from the world of imagination, sexuality, and whimsy. Cats' impact on the writers and artists of Paris has been far greater than that of dogs. Guy de Maupassant, J. K. Huysmans, and Anatole France all claimed to require the presence of a purring cat to conjure the muse. As Théophile Gautier wrote of his cat: "He shares your hours of work, solitude, of melancholy. He spends whole evenings on your knee, purring and dozing, content with your silence, and spurning for your sake the society of his kind." Victor Hugo wrote about his beloved Chanoine and Gavroche, while Colette called hers La Chatte Dernière (The Last Cat), even though many others were to follow. "There are no ordinary cats," said Colette, who always seemed to have one beside her as she wrote. After Colette introduced the surrealist filmmaker, poet, and artist Jean Cocteau to feline companionship, he saw the beasts as incarnations of the unconscious: "I love cats because I enjoy my home; and little by little, they become its visible soul. A kind of active silence emanates from these furry beasts who appear deaf to orders, to appeals, to approaches and who move in a completely royal authority." As the images in this book attest, French master photographers of the twentieth century–like Jacques-Henri Lartigue, Brassaï, Izis Bidermanus, and

4

Robert Doisneau—found the cat irresistible. A younger generation—including Marie Babey, Martine Franck, and Max Vadakul—has also been captivated by cats, which, unlike most pets, seem to need us less than we need them. Paris, a 2,500-year-old city, has a cat population that dates back to Roman times. In the sixth century A.D., King Childebert of France displayed a royal crest depicting a cat, yet cats were not always to live such charmed lives. Fear and superstition gave them a bad name in the Dark Ages: their mysterious, inscrutable ways led the populace to identify them with Satan, and they were ritually sacrificed on bonfires during the summer solstice festival of St. Jean the Baptist well into the eighteenth century. By the end of the fourteenth century, the European housecat had almost disappeared, and when ships returning from the Crusades imported rats carrying bubonic plague, nearly half of Europe died before rat-killing cats returned to save civilization. (As late as 1939, the National Printing Office of France employed a large staff of cats to guard the paper supply from the teeth of rats and mice.) Cats became favored pets of the bourgeoisie: one wealthy eighteenth-century gentleman had portraits painted of twenty-five of his cats. Yet during the 1871 Siege of Paris, the starving populace killed cats, cut off their paws and tails, and served them as ersatz rabbit stew. (When the ancient market Les Halles was destroyed in the 1970s to make way for the Centre Georges Pompidou, hundreds of cat skulls were found in the basement of an old butcher shop.) A cat lover is called an ailurophile. Alexander the Great, Napoleon, and Hitler were all ailurophobes, disliking the fickle uncontrollable nature of the feline. One of Napoleon's cat-loving enemies was the Vicomte de Chateaubriand, a statesman and the greatest author of his time in France, who lived with a big black-striped, greyish red cat. This cat led an extraordinary life, as

Chateaubriand recounted: "It was born in the Vatican, in the Raphael loggia. Leo XII brought it up in a fold of his robes where I had often looked at it enviously when the Pontiff gave me an audience." Known as The Pope's Cat, it enjoyed the "special consideration of pious ladies." When the Pope gave it to Chateaubriand, the author took it away from the pomp of the Vatican. "I am trying to make it forget exile, the Sistine Chapel, the sun on Michelangelo's cupola, where it used to walk, far above the earth." There are millions of cats in France today—no one knows exactly how many—and the number seems to be growing. In Paris, always a fanciful city, cats and their human companions play, wander, and dream, and, for the most part, modern cats do as they please. With about fifteen more vertebrae than a human spine, a cat's backbone has a flexibility of nearly 180 degrees, which allows it to play, leap, and twist in a way to have made Nureyev envious. Via its sixty-seven million olfactory cells, a cat smells things we can't even imagine. Unlike dogs, which revel in the more unpleasant odors of Paris streets, cats are as attracted to perfume and flower scents as they are to the aroma of a fish market. One of the oldest streets in the 6ème Arrondissement—really no more than a wide alley just off the Seine—is called La Rue du Chat Qui Pêche (Street of the Cat Who Fishes). A cat spends about two-thirds of its life sleeping and the other third eating, preening, playing, and making love. In the ballet *Les Demoiselles de la Nuit* by Roland Pétit and Jean Anouilh, a cat called Agathe falls in love with a man. Their love is a tricky one, and when Agathe flees he follows her across the roofs of Paris, only to plunge to his death. In the end, heartsick, Agathe returns to die at his side. And anyone who has lived in Paris and been awakened at midnight to caterwauling will appreciate the fact that Maurice Ravel's children's opera, *L'Enfant et les Sortilèges* (based on a story by Colette), contains a duet for a male and female cat. Georges-Louis Leclerc, the Comte de Buffon, was France's premier naturalist in the eighteenth century and the author of the monumental *Histoire naturelle*. Buffon detested cats, considering them lazy, conniving animals, "untrustworthy servants" that one kept only to rid the household of rodents. "They take easily to the habits of society, but never to its moral attitudes; they only appear to be affectionate." Buffon noted that the female cat, roaming the rooftops at night, was more ardent than the male to achieve sexual satisfaction: "She invites it, calls for it, announces her desires by her piercing cries, or rather, the excess of her needs." A century later, Alphonse Toussenel in his book *Zoologie passionelle* saw in cats a direct reflection of human sexual relations, drawing a link with women of easy virtue. "An animal who makes the night her day, and who shocks decent people with the noises of her orgies, can only have one single analogy in this world, and that analogy is of the feminine kind." Perhaps the fact that cats were viewed as such highly sexual and immoral—or at least amoral—creatures was the reason why poet Charles Baudelaire loved them so: "Come, superb cat, to my amorous heart; Hold back the talons of your paws." Baudelaire's mistress, Jeanne Duval, banished his beloved cat, replacing it with a dog, because she knew how he hated them. (Years later, however, when he was in his Belgian exile, Baudelaire grew to admire dogs so much he wrote a poem called "*Les bons chiens*.") Because of their nocturnal habits and insouciant ways, cats became symbols of witchcraft, sexual liberty, and the artists and intellectuals who lived on the margins of society. "The cat lives alone, has no need of society, does not obey except when it likes, pretends to sleep that it may see the more clearly, and scratches everything that it can scratch," wrote Chateaubriand. As Théophile Gautier wrote: "It is no easy task to win the friendship of a cat…. He does not bestow his regard lightly, and, though he may consent to be your companion, he will never be your slave." Cats—like humans—vary tremendously in their capacity for emotional attachments. In her fine book *The Beast in the Boudoir*, Kathleen Kete tells how Catulle Mendès owned a cat that killed himself after being neutered. When Mendès brought him back from the veterinarian, "Mime fell into a depression blacker than his beautiful velvet coat." One morning, the cat threw himself from the window ledge and fell to the street, where he broke his back. "I have the distinct impression that Mime committed suicide," commented the author. Then there is Morrill Cody's tale that, when Modigliani died, the cat that had been his most faithful friend jumped out of the window of his studio, killing itself at the very moment that the painter expired at the hospital. (Shortly afterward the artist's young wife jumped from the sixth-floor window of her hotel.) "Our perfect companions never have fewer than four feet," wrote Colette. What strange bond is formed between human and feline? Anyone who has loved a cat and lost it will appreciate Gautier's poignant elegy, which embraces our own mortality: "Dynasties of cats, as numerous as the dynasties of the Pharaohs, succeeded each other under my roof. One after the other they were swept away by accident, by flight, by death. All were loved and regretted; but oblivion is our common fate, and the memory of the cats we have lost fades like the memory of men." It seems no coincidence to me that Père LaChaise Cemetery, filled with the graves of geniuses like Modigliani, Chopin, Balzac, Delacroix, Proust, and Edith Piaf, should be populated by several hundred feral cats, who roam among the tombs like spirits, surviving on birds, rats, and handouts from doddering old cat ladies. In Paris, as François Fossier wrote, "Cats are forever."

MY CAT DOES NOT
TALK AS RESPECTFULLY
TO ME AS I DO TO HER.
{ Colette }

21

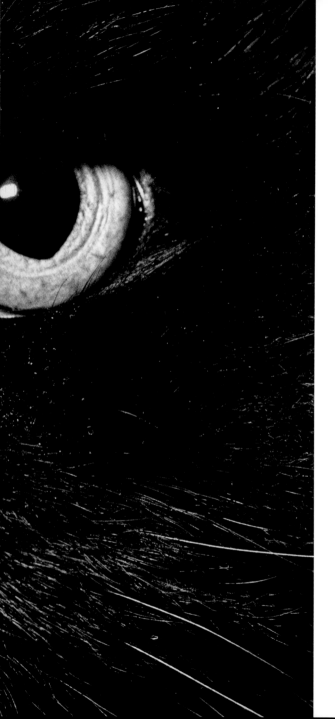

LIKE THOSE
GREAT SPHINXES LOUNGING
THROUGH ETERNITY IN
NOBLE ATTITUDES UPON THE
DESERT SAND, THEY GAZE
INCURIOUSLY AT NOTHING,
CALM AND WISE.
{ Charles Baudelaire }

36

45

47

HE SHARES YOUR
HOURS OF WORK, SOLITUDE,
OF MELANCHOLY. HE SPENDS
WHOLE EVENINGS ON YOUR KNEE,
PURRING AND DOZING, CONTENT
WITH YOUR SILENCE, AND
SPURNING FOR YOUR SAKE THE
SOCIETY OF HIS KIND.
{ Théophile Gautier }

EVEN IN HIS MOST
AFFECTIONATE MOODS HE
PRESERVES HIS FREEDOM,
AND REFUSES A SERVILE
OBEDIENCE. BUT ONCE GAIN
HIS CONFIDENCE, AND HE
IS A FRIEND FOR LIFE.
{ Théophile Gautier }

LES CHATS
de Paris

{ Credits }

3 ©Walter Limot, *La main de Colette*, c.1940 (Rapho)

9 Jacques Henri Lartigue, *Les Jumeaux, Paris, Mars, 1908* (©Association des Amis de J. H. Lartigue, Paris)

10 ©Pierre Michaud, *Une fillette et son chat à la fenêtre*, 1975 (Rapho)

11 ©Jean-Noël De Soye, *Marion et son chat*, 1986 (Rapho)

12 ©Marie Babey, *Virgile et Julien à la fenêtre*, 1990 (Photo Marie Babey, Paris)

13 ©Marie Babey, *A tu et à toit, Ingrid et Virgile*, 1989 (Photo Marie Babey, Paris)

14 ©Martine Franck, *Métro*, 1977 (Magnum)

15 Brassaï, *Le chat du bistrot*, 1944 (©Gilberte Brassaï, Paris)

16 ©Robert Doisneau, *Rue des Beaux Arts*, 1953 (Rapho)

17 ©Marie Babey, *L'heure du Berger, Quai de Jemmapes*, 1990 (Photo Marie Babey, Paris)

18 ©Martine Franck, *Chat blanc à la vitrine*, 1984 (Magnum)

19 Brassaï, *La modiste*, c.1935 (©Gilberte Brassaï, Paris)

20 ©Sanford Roth, *Colette*, c.1950 (Rapho)

22 ©Pierre Darnoc, *Le rendezvous I*, 1986

23 ©Pierre Darnoc, *Le rendezvous II*, 1986

24 ©Robert Doisneau, *Maison Lavirotte, 29 Avenue Rapp*, 1982 (Rapho)

25 ©Willy Ronis, *Le chat de la concierge*, 1947 (Rapho)

26 ©Henri Cartier-Bresson, *Les chats de Leonor Fini*, 1960 (Magnum)

27 ©Robert Doisneau, *Concierge parisienne*, 1945 (Rapho)

28 ©Max Vadukul, *Fric-frac, Paris*, 1992 (Art + Commerce, New York)

29 ©Max Vadukul, *Romeo Gigli, Paris*, 1994 (Art + Commerce, New York)

30 ©Marie Babey, *Allez Virgile! Canal Saint Martin*, 1989 (Photo Marie Babey, Paris)

31 ©Martine Franck, *Cimetière du Père LaChaise*, 1984 (Magnum)

32 André Kertész, *Rue Bourgeois*, 1931 (©Ministère de la Culture)

33 André Kertész, *Port Saint-Denis*, 1928 (©Ministère de la Culture)

34 ©Richard Phelps, *Les yeux*, 1985 (Rapho)

36 André Kertész, *Le Chat du studio*, c.1926 (©Ministère de la Culture)

37 ©Marie Babey, *Virgile, le Bucolique*, 1991 (Photo Marie Babey, Paris)

38 ©Edouard Boubat, *La Partition*, 1982 (Rapho)

39 ©Janine Nièpce, *Un chat et une guitare*, 1952 (Rapho)

40 ©Pierre Darnoc, *Les musiciens*, 1993

41 ©Jean-Marc Charles, *Restaurant de Poissons*, 1987 (Rapho)

42 Brassaï, *Au chat qui pelote*, 1939 (©Gilberte Brassaï, Paris)

43 ©Charlie Abad, *Métro-clodo-dodo*, 1978 (Photo Charlie Abad, Paris)

44 Anonymous, *Foujita*, 1927 (©Collection Viollet, Roger-Viollet, Paris)

45 Bonnot, *Louis Coulon et sa barbe de 3.5 metres*, 1904, (©Fotofolio, New York, A. N. Ulrich Collection)

46 Izis (Izis Bidermanus), *Jacques Prévert, terrasse d'un café à Paris*, 1949 (©Photo Izis, Paris)

47 René-Jacques, *Léon-Paul Fargue*, 1937 (©Ministère de la Culture)

48 ©Hervé Gloaguen, *Jean Cocteau*, 1962 (Rapho)

49 ©Sanford Roth, *Blaise Cendrars*, c.1950 (Rapho)

50 ©Hélene Adant, *Henri Matisse*, 1949 (Rapho)

52 ©Marie Babey, *Maurice et Pif, Restaurant Le Bourgogne, rue des Vinaigriers*, 1995 (Photo Marie Babey, Paris)

53 Brassaï, *Le chat blanc au cellier*, c.1946 (©Gilberte Brassaï, Paris)

54 Izis (Izis Bidermanus), *Près du Jardin du Luxembourg*, 1950 (©Photo Izis, Paris)

55 ©Josef Koudelka, *Les partenaires*, 1983 (Magnum)

56 ©Robert Doisneau, *Le plus beau chat de l'exposition*, 1946 (Rapho)

57 ©Robert Doisneau, *Le paradis des chats*, 1950 (Rapho)

58 Brassaï, *Les petits équilibristes*, c.1930 (©Gilberte Brassaï, Paris)

59 Brassaï, *Un dresseur de la rue*, c.1930 (©Gilberte Brassaï, Paris)

60 Anonymous, *Georges Brassens chez lui*, 1957 (©Collection Viollet, Roger-Viollet, Paris)

61 ©Emmanuelle Jacquot, *Pouchkine*, 1991 (Photo Jacquot, Paris)

62 ©Winston Conrad, *Les Amis du Pont des Arts*, 1993 (Photo Winston Conrad, San Francisco)

64 ©Jean-Marc Charles, *Minou fait la manche pour payer ses frais vétérinaires*, 1981 (Rapho)

65 ©Marc Riboud, *La clinique pour animaux, rue de Bièvres, 9ème Arrondissement*, 1953 (Magnum)

66 ©Agnès Chaumat, *Léon*, 1976 (Rapho)

67 ©Pierre Darnoc, *Perdu? Volé?*, 1993

68 ©Willy Ronis, *La fenêtre* 1954 (Rapho)

This book was designed by Jilly Simons with Susan Carlson at Concrete, Chicago, Illinois. The text was set in Bernhard Modern, designed by Lucian Bernhard, 1938, Chevalier, designed by E. A. Neukomm, 1946, and Cochin, designed by Matthew Carter, 1977, based on the original by Sol Hess, 1917. The book was printed in Singapore.